POSTCARDS FROM SANTA LAND

Joe Pascoe

POSTCARDS FROM SANTA LAND

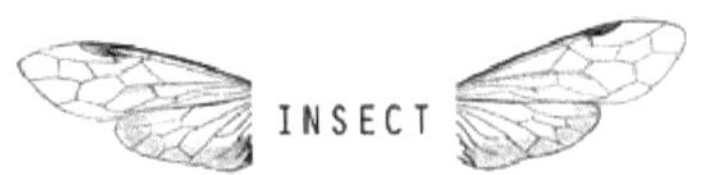

Acknowledgements

My love to Lyndel Wischer, Eve Pascoe and John Pascoe.
Curatorial Research by Zoe Constantinou'
Cover: Christmas postcard 1, collage, Joe Pascoe 2021
My continuing appreciation goes to the NDIS (Adam Bos).

Contents

Preface

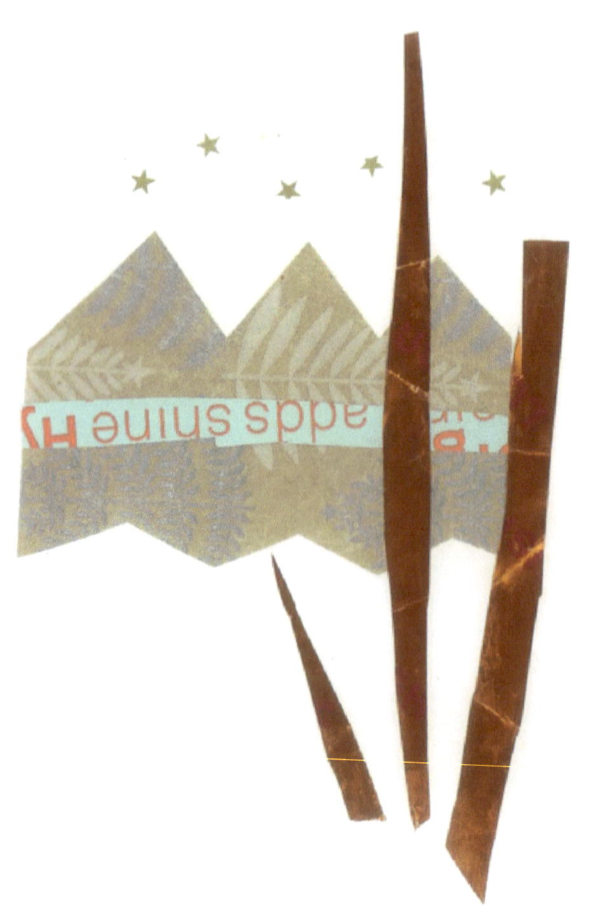
adds shine Hy

Preface

Most of these collages were made from used Christmas
wrapping paper, once lovingly wrapped around gifts. I
gathered up the happy debris of the day and took it
home.

Over the next few days I relived their beauty. The
collages came easily and taped into warm, rich feelings.
The poems appeared progressively as part of my general
writing.

I hope you enjoy 'Postcards from Santa Land'.

Joe Pascoe

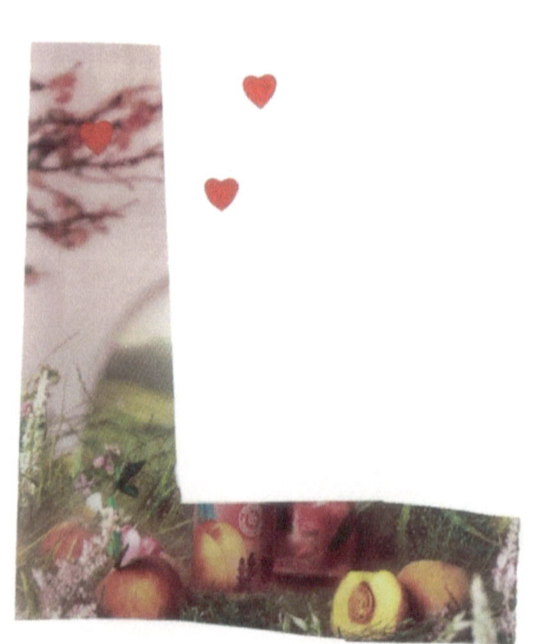

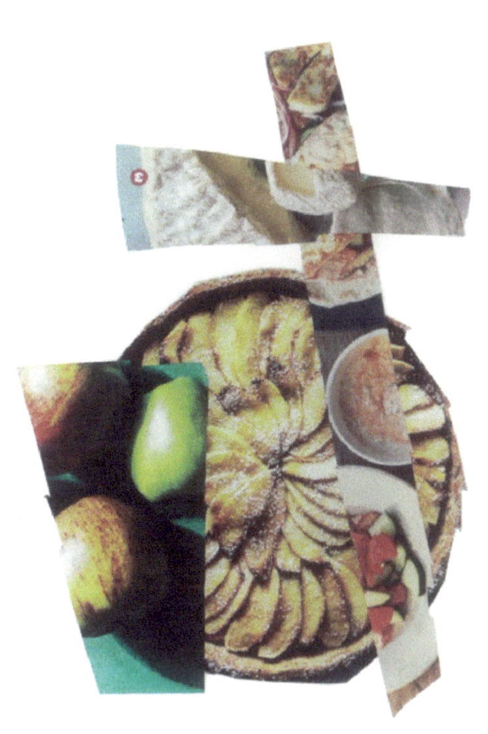

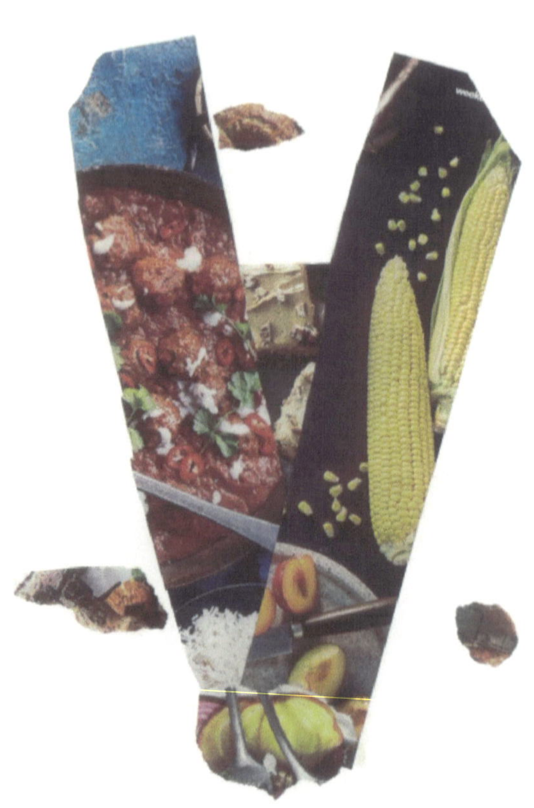

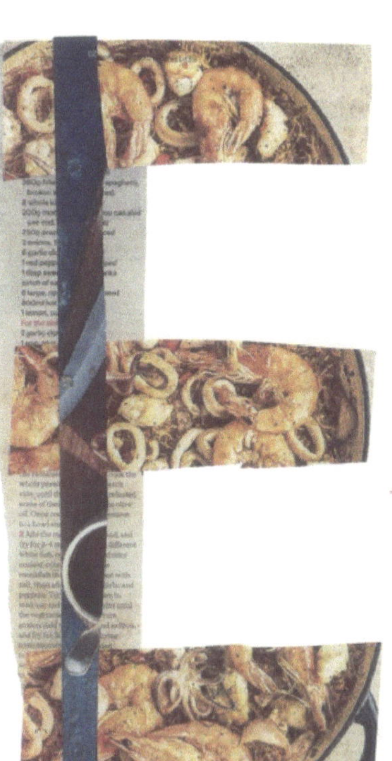

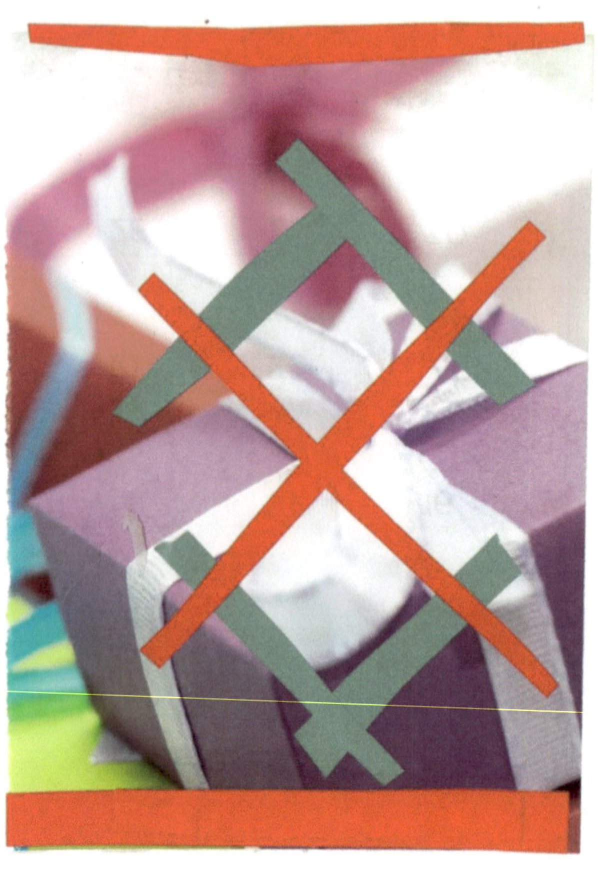

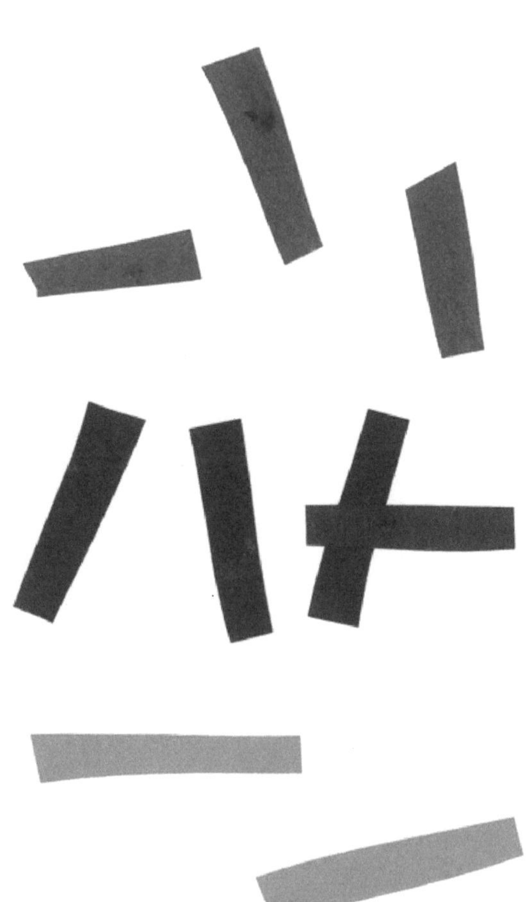

Santa Land

Santa land is sweet like honey
Real bees and flowers

Their dreams, your dreams
Lifting grey skies away

I believe
I feel it
We put up our Christmas tree
It's familiarity a treat
Electrifying the past
Kids were small
Smiles so broad

Feeling proud of ourselves
Loving the lights
Going to church, often
A beautiful lunch
Rum butter on pudding
Then santa comes

It's for everyone
Say happy christmas in the street
Give the dog a treat

Chill right down
Put away the frown
Do it well
It will make you swell
laugh with love
Oh magic santa land.

Email laying on the street

Man on the street
Sleeping bag covering his feet
Why there?
It does not seem fair

Alone on the hard dirt
A thousand pass him by
He does not cry

I treat you like an email
A glance, a thought
Dispelled, deleted

Just this poem to atone
I hope you feel the love

It's a good plan.

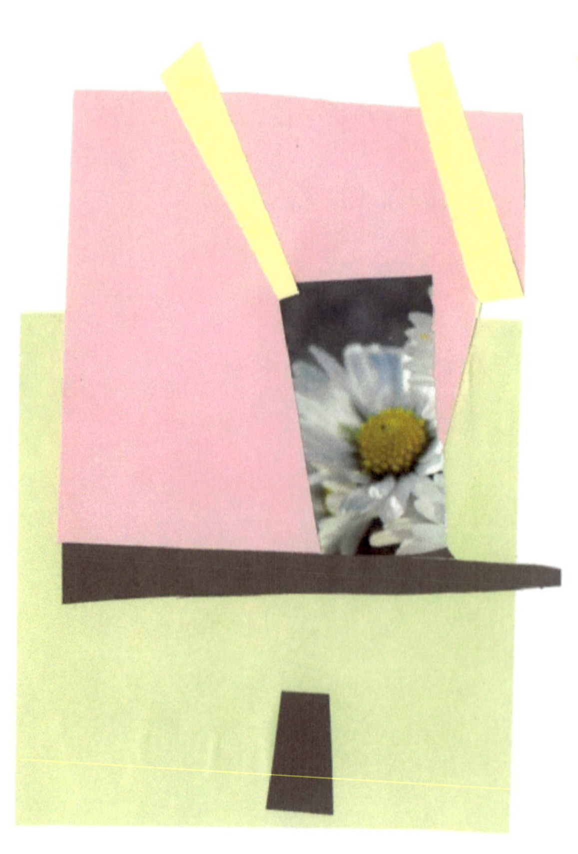

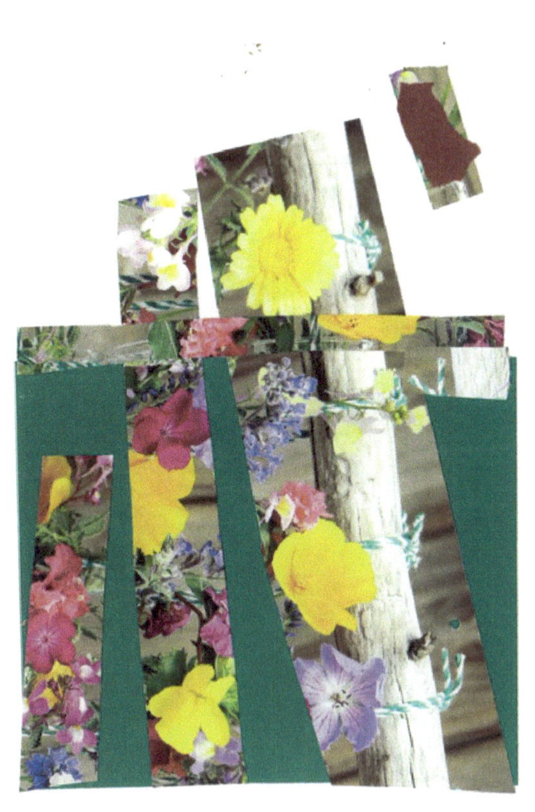

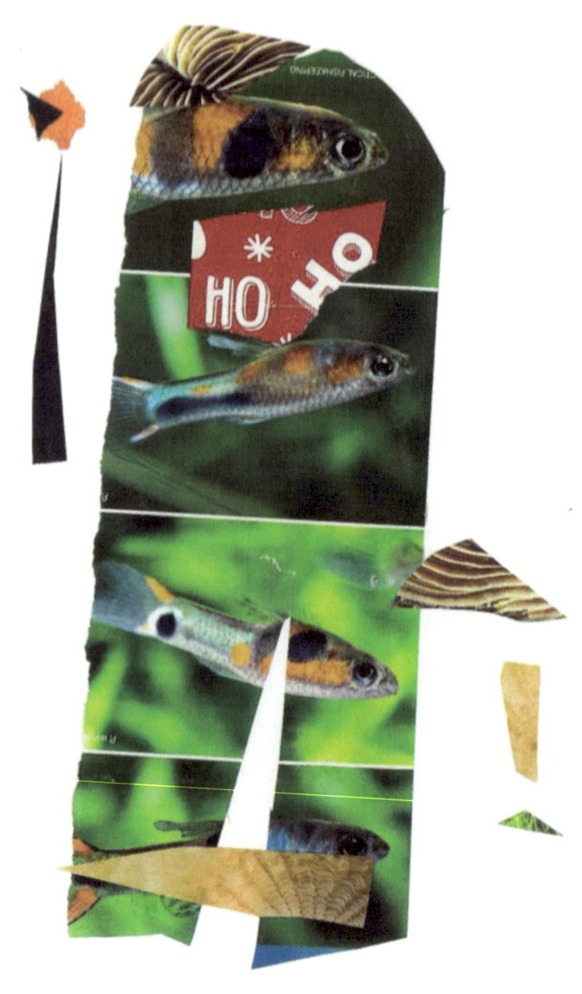
HO HO

New Year fish gods

Fish gods in the sea
Floating free
Attached to thee
I see you and want to spawn
Our eggs to mingle
More fish to come

Deep, deep in the ocean
Or lazing in a pond
Rushing down a stream
We fish gods like to dream

Sun breaks through
Rain comes down
Spring leaves spin around

And all abounds.

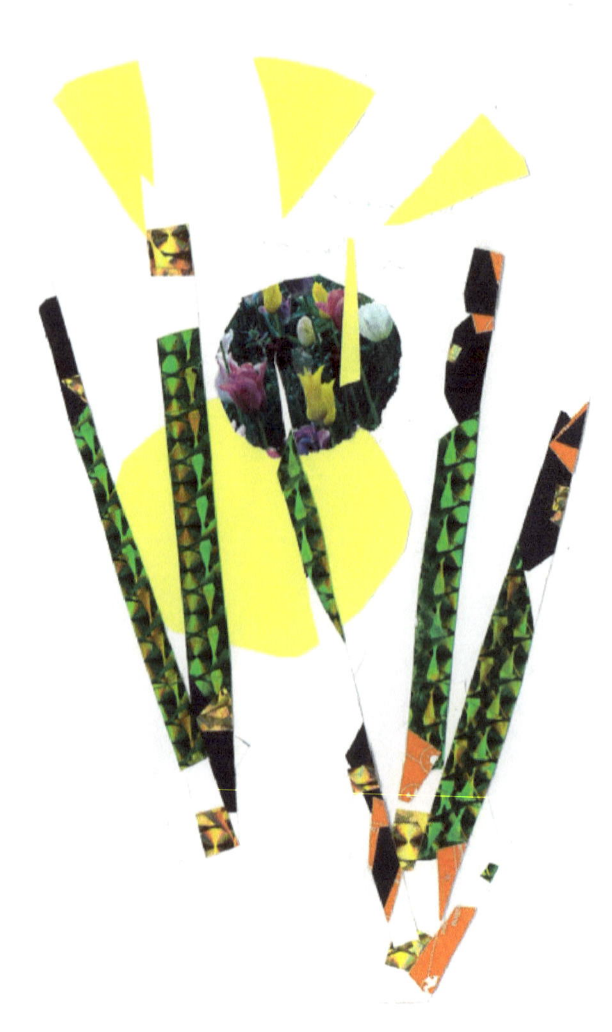

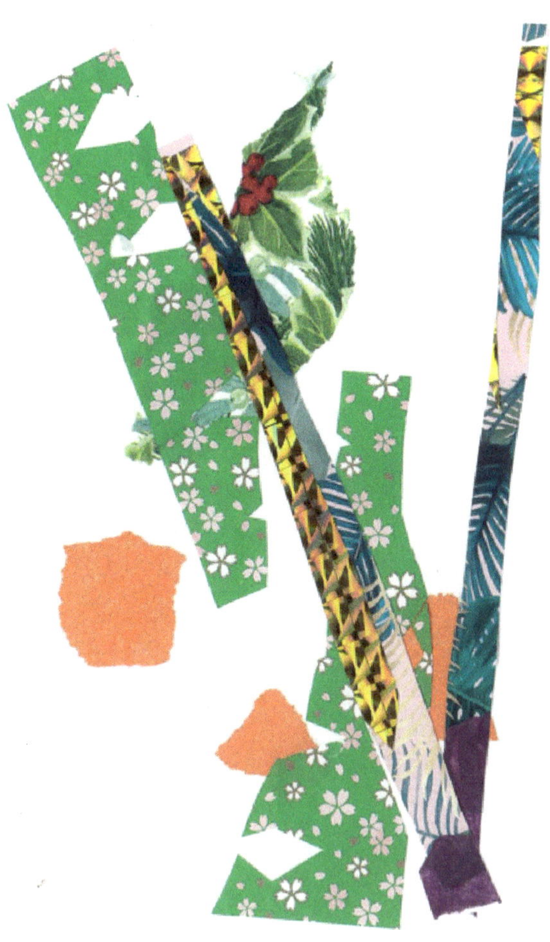

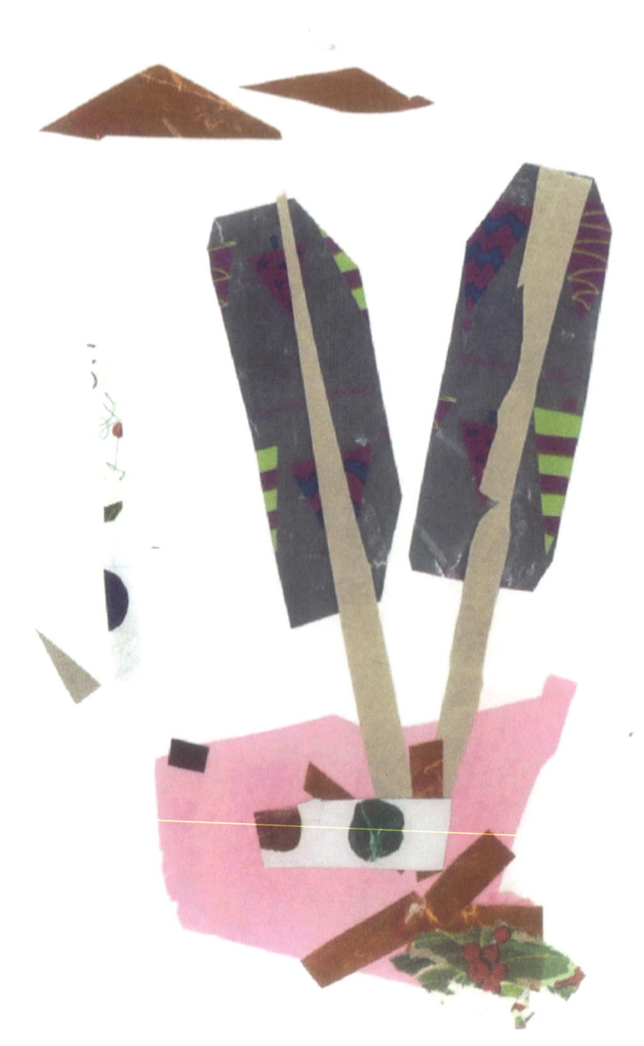

Hoping for a puppy

The snow is made of lemonade
Fairy gloss clouds float by
Church bells sing a ding ding

Children come out to play
Bats and balls
Boys calling out imaginary scores

Old women put down their knitting
They remember their own beginnings
That boy I wanted to kiss
Ponytails all astray
Aunties they loved
Pesky little sisters they may have shoved

Nothing too real
Love was gay
Innocence was still the way
Books to read
Little Tommy peed
The man holding the Bible was kind
Telling the story of the Christ child
Be kind to all he cried
I let out a gentle sigh
Promised myself not to poke poor Tommy in the eye

Offering plate went around
Someone had put in a pound
My sixpence clattered in
Rolling around with a cheeky grin
It flopped down
I sat down
And waited for life to begin.

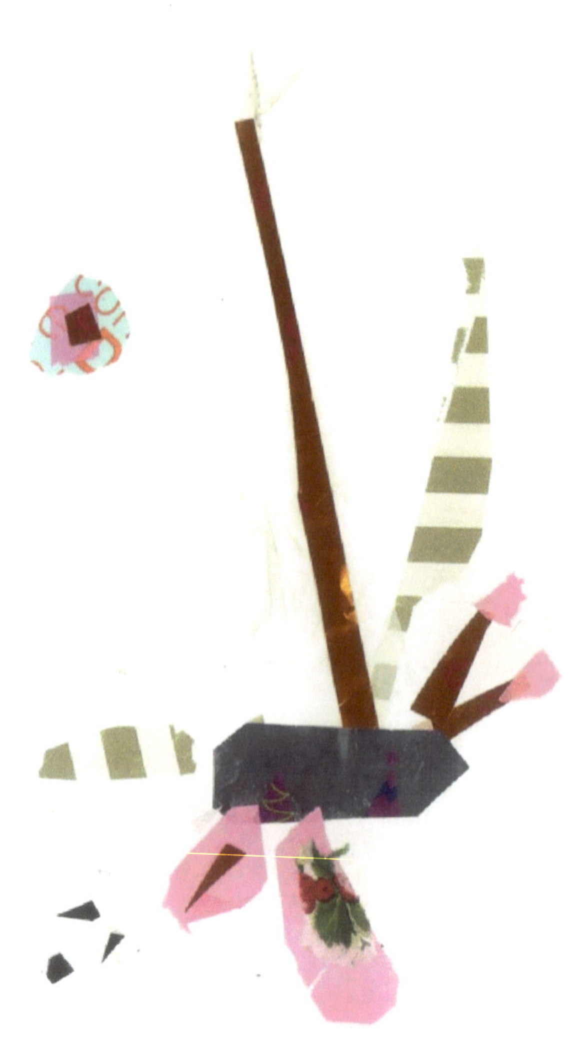

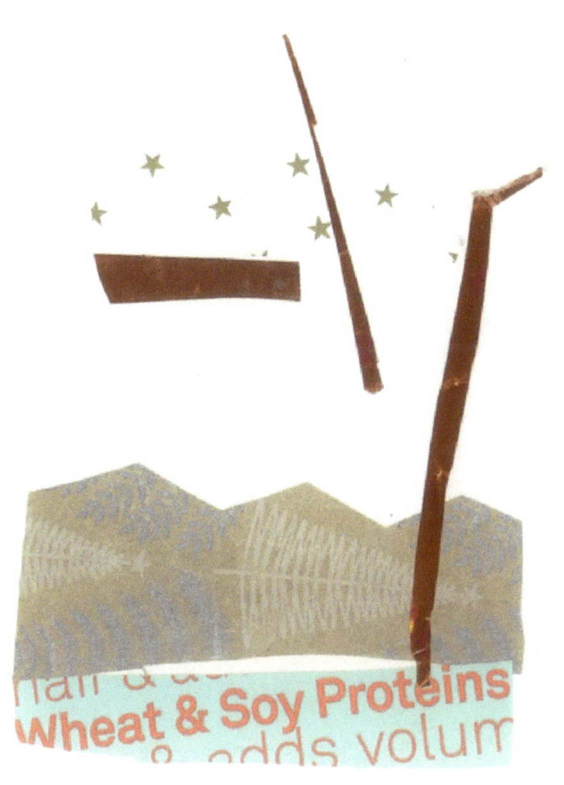
Wheat & Soy Proteins
& adds volum

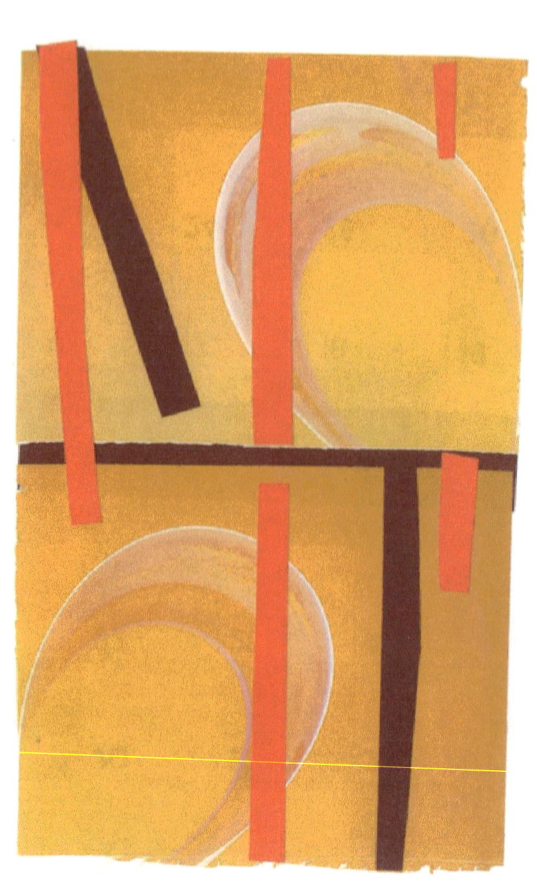

Amen

Grace
I like it when someone says grace
A simple thank you for the food we are to taste
Elbows in, knees clean
Adults and children breathe in
Everyone quiet, we can now begin.

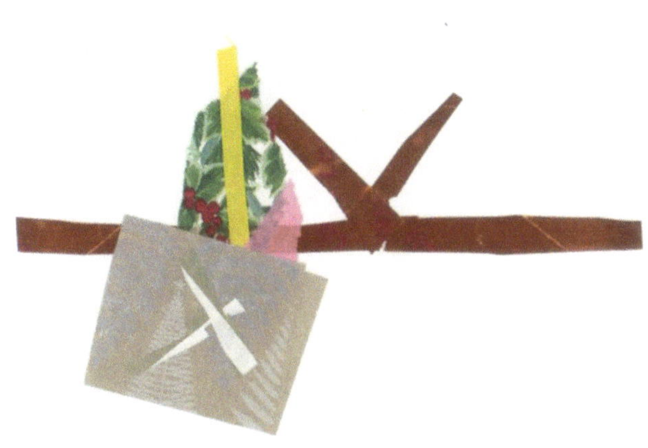

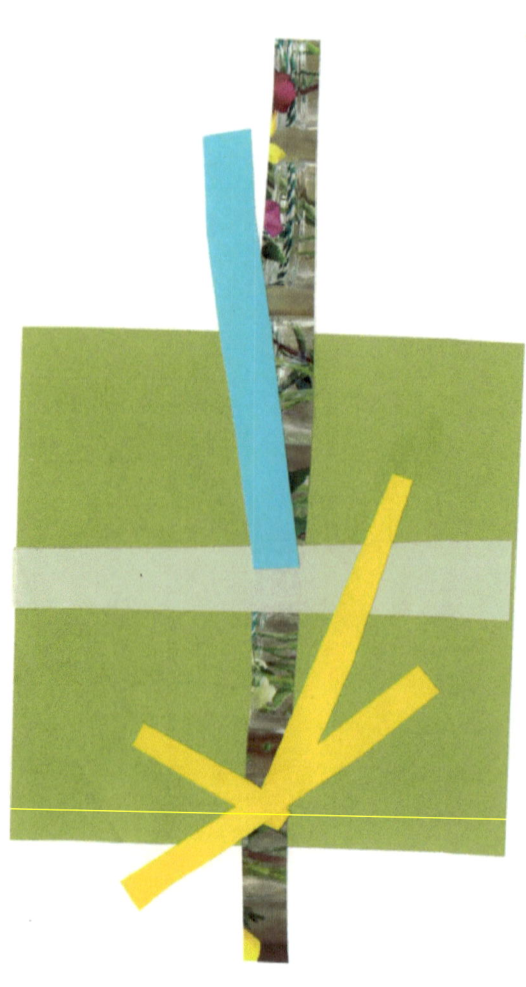

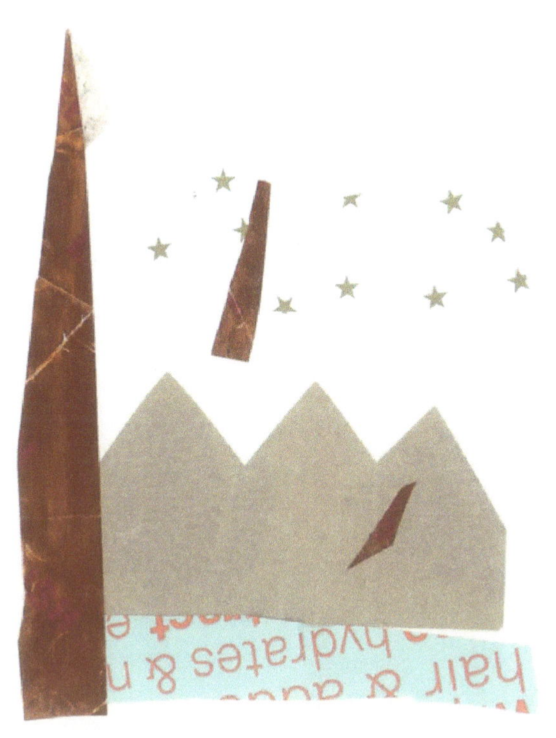

hair &
hydrates & n

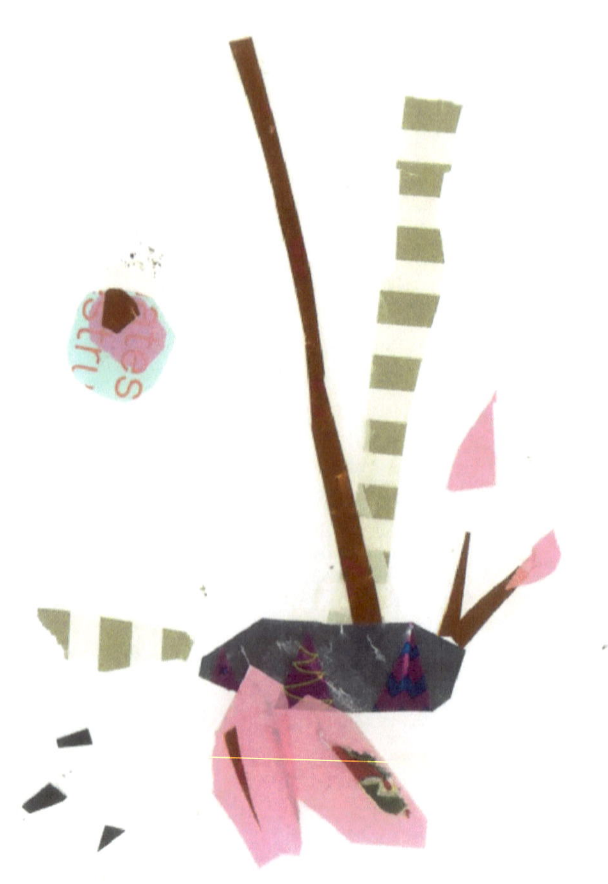

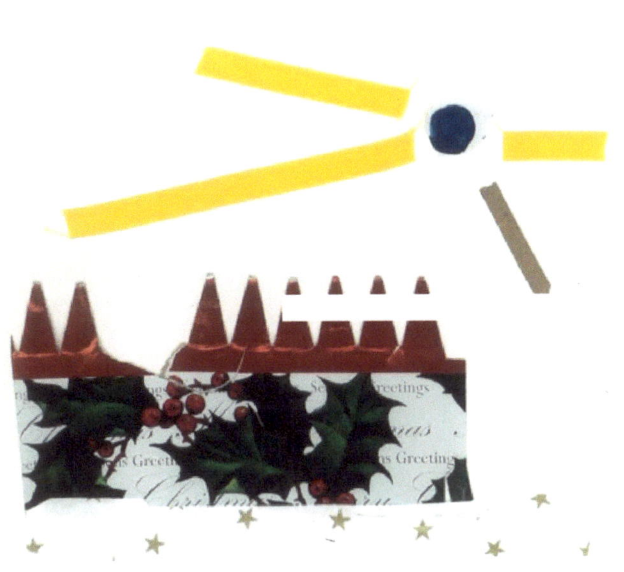

9 780645 886719